GW00499750

Other books by Robert Kraus and N. M. Bodecker
GOOD NIGHT RICHARD RABBIT
GOOD NIGHT LITTLE ONE

FIRST PUBLISHED IN GREAT BRITAIN 1974
REISSUED 1989
TEXT COPYRIGHT © 1972 ROBERT KRAUS
ILLUSTRATIONS COPYRIGHT © 1972 N. M. BODECKER

JONATHAN CAPE LTD, 32 BEDFORD SQUARE, LONDON WC1B 3SG

ISBN 0 224 01022 0

PRINTED IN GREAT BRITAIN
BY MACLEHOSE & PARTNERS LTD, PORTSMOUTH

ROBERT KRAUS

GOOD NIGHT

LITTLE A·B·C

N. M. BODECKER

JONATHAN CAPE
THIRTY-TWO BEDFORD SQUARE
LONDON

A a

Good Night Little A
Alfred Alvin Alligator
Good Night Little A

Good Night Little B
Bertram Bullfinch Basset Hound
Good Night Little B

Cc

Good Night Little C
Celia Cynthia Crane
Good Night Little C

Dd

Good Night Little D
David Daniel Dormouse
Good Night Little D

E e

Good Night Little E
Edward Elmer Elephant
Good Night Little E

Ff

Good Night Little F
Flora Felicity Fawn
Good Night Little F

Gg

Good Night Little G
Gregory Guggenheim Guinea Pig
Good Night Little G

Hh

Good Night Little H
Hilary Haggerty Hedgehog
Good Night Little H

I i

**Good Night Little I
Igor Illych Iguana
Good Night Little I**

J j

Good Night Little J
Jasper Jabber Jay
Good Night Little J

K k

Good Night Little K
Kevin Kasper Kangaroo
Good Night Little K

L l

Good Night Little L
Leo Limehouse Lion
Good Night Little L

M m

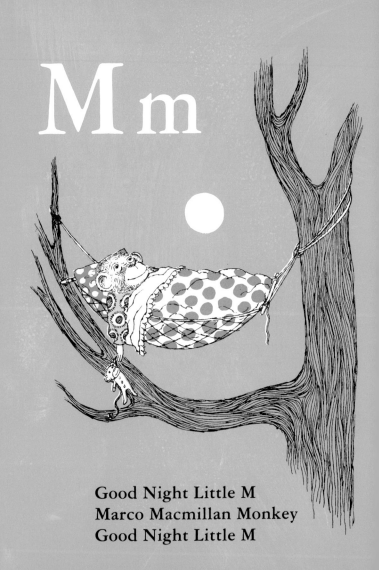

Good Night Little M
Marco Macmillan Monkey
Good Night Little M

N n

Good Night Little N
Norman Nicholas Natterjack
Good Night Little N

Good Night Little O
Olga Ophelia Owl
Good Night Little O

P p

Good Night Little P
Perry Ponsonby Penguin
Good Night Little P

Qq

Good Night Little Q
Quillian Quorry Quail
Good Night Little Q

Rr

Good Night Little R
Richard Robinson Rabbit
Good Night Little R

Ss

Good Night Little S
Samson Simonson Shrimp
Good Night Little S

Tt

Good Night Little T
Thomas Tarkington Tadpole
Good Night Little T

Uu

**Good Night Little U
Uncas Uranus Unicorn
Good Night Little U**

V v

Good Night Little V
Vera Veronica Vixen
Good Night Little V

W w

Good Night Little W
Wilbur Worthington Worm
Good Night Little W

Xx

**Good Night Little X
Xenophon Xerxes Xiphosura*
Good Night Little X**

*horseshoe crab, that is

Yy

Good Night Little Y
Yelva Yacobowsky Yak
Good Night Little Y

Zz

**Good Night Little Z
Zorba Zachary Zebra
Good Night Little Z-Z-Z-Z-Z-z-z-z-z-z**